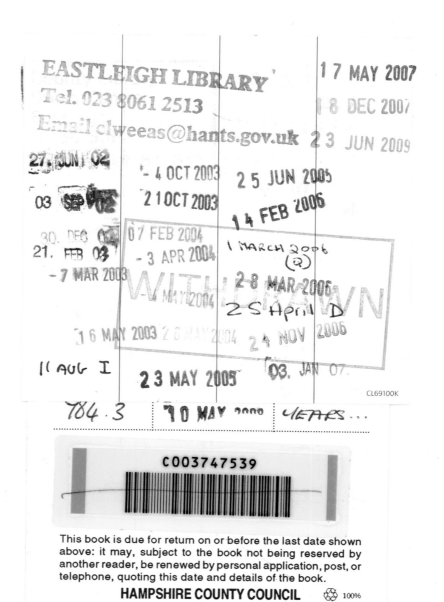

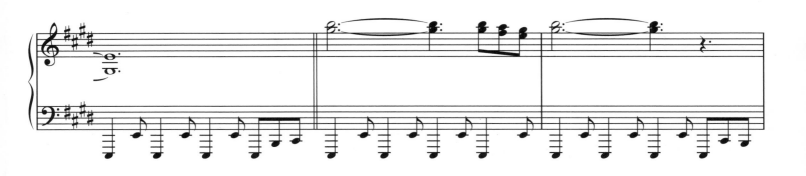

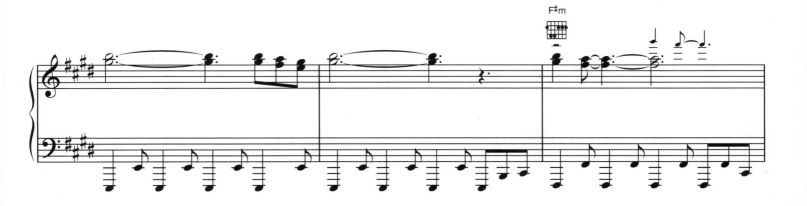

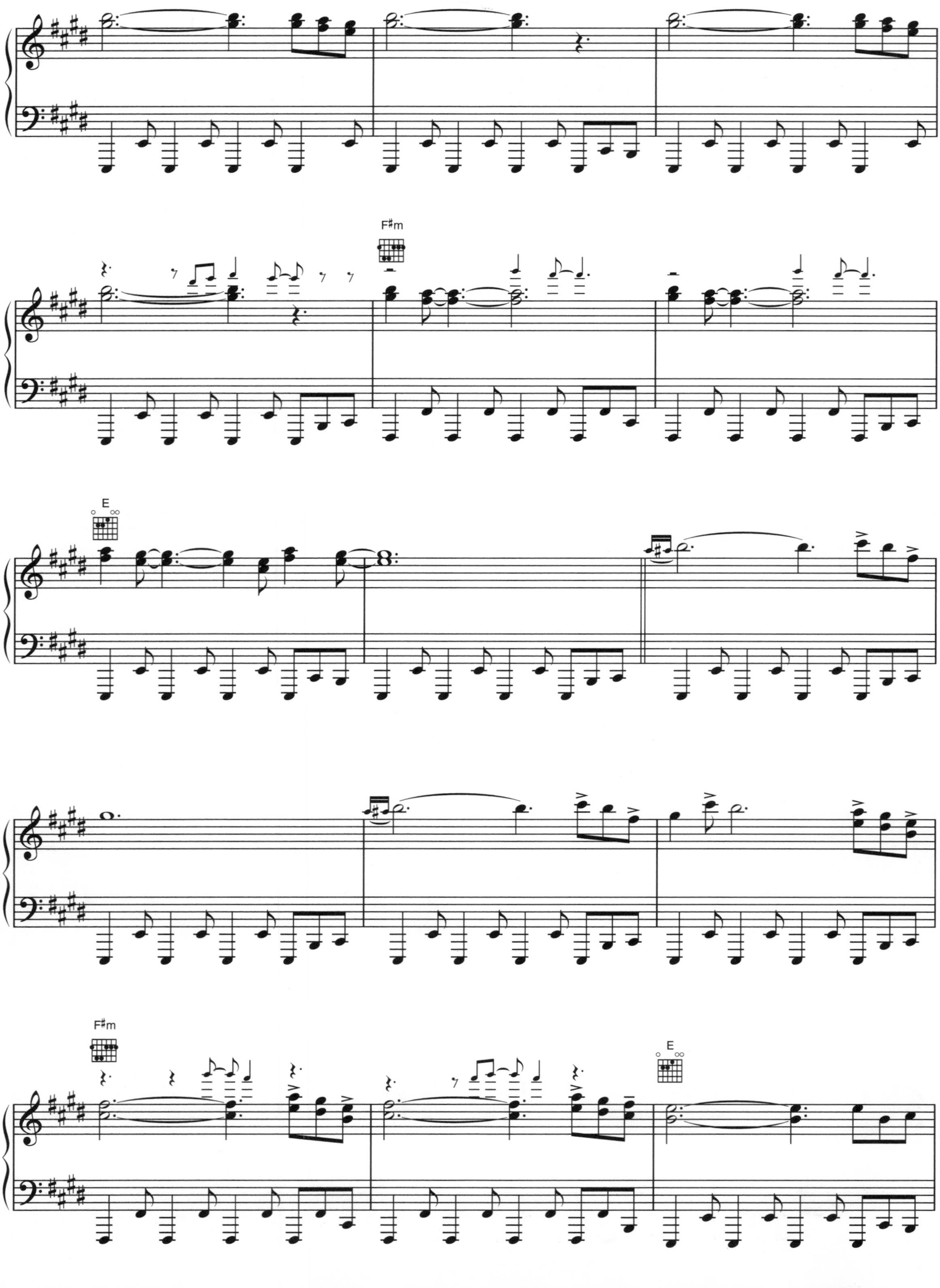
F♯m
E
F♯m
E

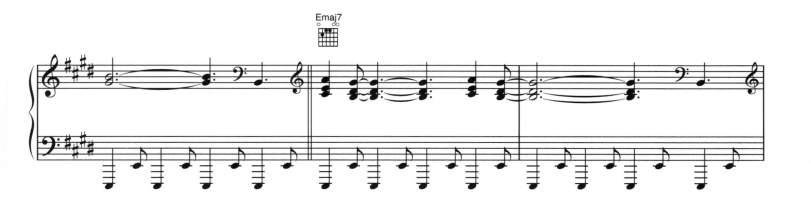
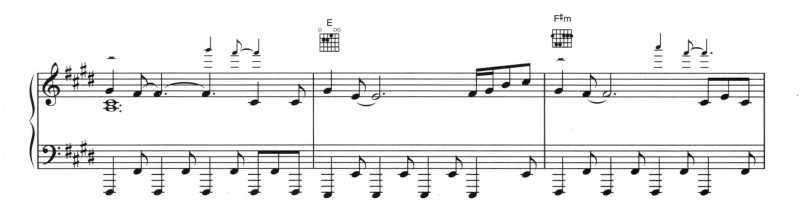

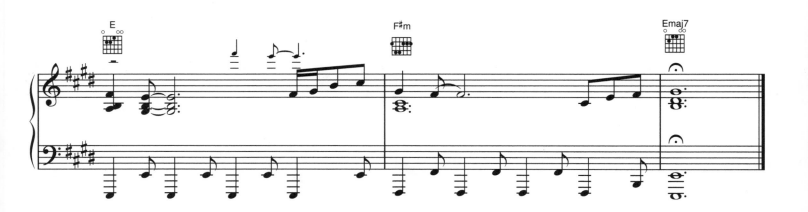

BABY LOVE

Words and Music by BRIAN HOLLAND, EDDIE HOLLAND
and LAMONT DOZIER

don't you stay, need you, need you, ba-by love, ooh,—

ba – by love.

D. %. al Coda

CODA

Ooh,— ooh,— need to hold you— once a-

BIG GIRLS DON'T CRY

Words and Music by BOB CREWE and BOB GAUDIO

CALIFORNIA GIRLS

Words and Music by BRIAN WILSON and MIKE LOVE

girls.

I

wish thay all could be Ca - li - for - nia; I wish they all could be

Ca - li - for - nia; I Ca - li - for - nia girls.

FROM RUSSIA WITH LOVE

Words and Music by LIONEL BART

FIRE AND RAIN

Words and Music by JAMES TAYLOR

Just yes-ter-day morn-in' they let me know— you were gone,

Su-san, the plans they made put an end to you. I walked out this morn-in' and I

wrote down this song,— I just can't re-mem-ber who to send it to.

Verse 2:

Won't you look down upon me, Jesus, you got to help me make a stand
You just got to see me through another day
My body's achin' and my time is at hand
An' I won't make it any other way

Verse 3:

Been walkin' my mind to an easy time, my back turned towards the sun
Lord knows when the cold wind blows it'll turn your head around
Well, there's hours of time on the telephone line, to talk about things to come
Sweet dreams and flying machines in pieces on the ground

FOR ONCE IN MY LIFE

Words by RONALD MILLER
Music by ORLANDO MURDEN

25

FUN, FUN, FUN

Words and Music by MIKE LOVE and BRIAN WILSON

Well, she

HE WAS REALLY SAYIN' SOMETHING

Words and Music by NORMAN WHITFIELD, EDDIE HOLLAND
and WILLIAMSON STEVENSON

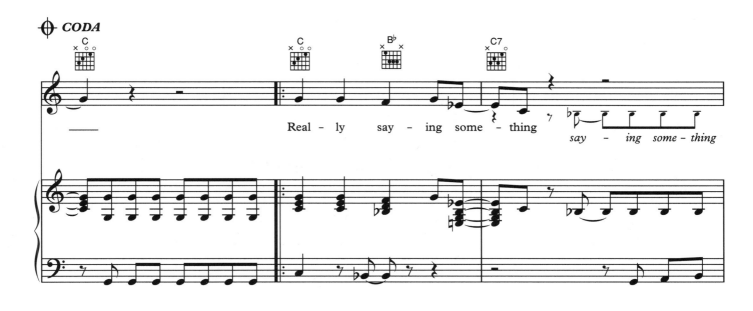

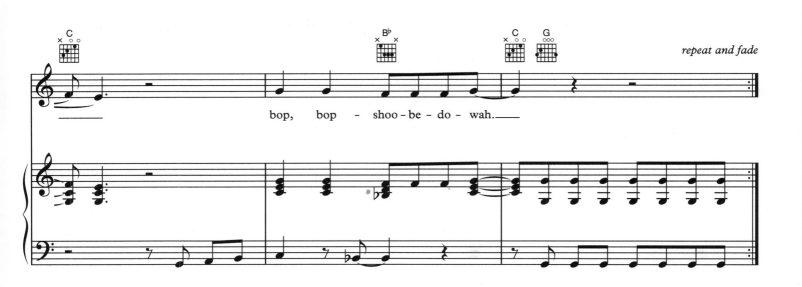

THE HOUSE THAT JACK BUILT

Words and Music by BOB LANCE and FRAN ROBBINS

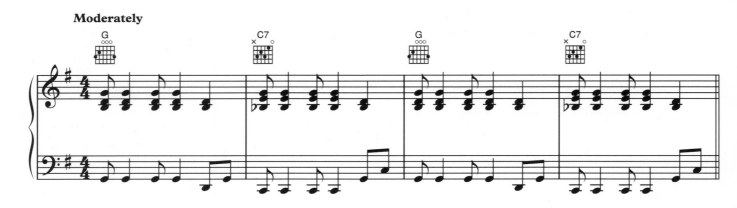

This was the land— that he worked by hand, it was the dream for an up-right man,
There was a fence— that held our love, there was a gate— that he walked out of.

there was a room— that was filled with love, it was the love— that I walked out of.
This is a heart— and it turned to stone, this is a house, it ain't no home.

IT TAKES TWO

Words and Music by SYLVIA MOY and WILLIAM STEVENSON

One can have a dream ba-by, two can make that dream so real.

One can talk a-bout be - ing in love. Two can say how it real-ly feels.

One can wish up-on a star, two can make that wish come true.

just takes two,——

Verse 2:

One can have a broken heart, living in misery
Two can really ease the pain like the perfect remedy
One can be alone in a crowd, like an island he's all alone
Two can make it just-a any place seem just like being home

Verse 3:

One can go out to a movie, looking for a special treat
Two can make that-a single movie something really kind-a sweet
One can take a walk in the moonlight, thinking that it's really nice
Ah but two walking a-hand in hand is like adding just a pinch of spice

ITCHYCOO PARK

Words and Music by STEVE MARRIOTT and RONNIE LANE

DRUG ADDICT'S SONG

Moderately

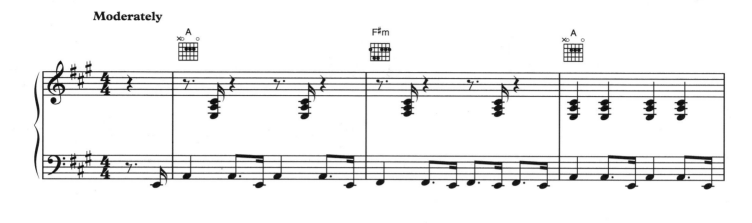

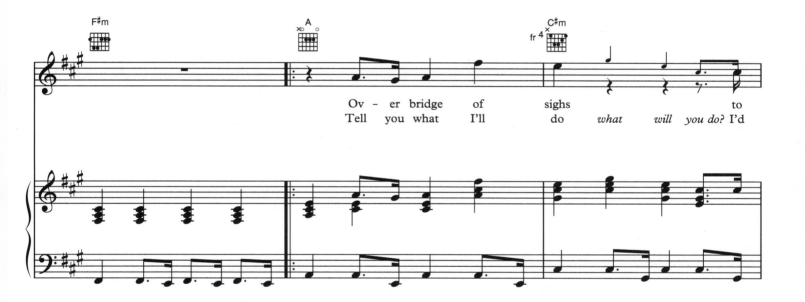

Ov - er bridge of sighs to
Tell you what I'll do *what will you do?* I'd

rest my eyes in shades of green. Un - der dream - ing
like to go there now with you. You can miss out

THE LOOK OF LOVE

Words by HAL DAVID
Music by BURT BACHARACH

46

Verse 2:
You've got the look of love, it's on your face
A look that time can't erase
Be mine tonight, let this be just the start
Of so many nights like this
Let's take a lover's vow
And then seal it with a kiss

Verse 3: (Instrumental)

LET'S DANCE

Words and Music by JIM LEE

Hey ba-by won't you take a chance. Say that you'll let me
Hey ba-by yeah you thrill me so.___ Hold me tight don't you

have this dance, let's dance, let's dance,
let me go,___ let's dance,

We'll do the twist, the stomp, the mashed po-ta-to too.___

MAKE SOMEONE HAPPY

Words by BETTY COMDEN and ADOLPH GREEN
Music by JULE STYNE

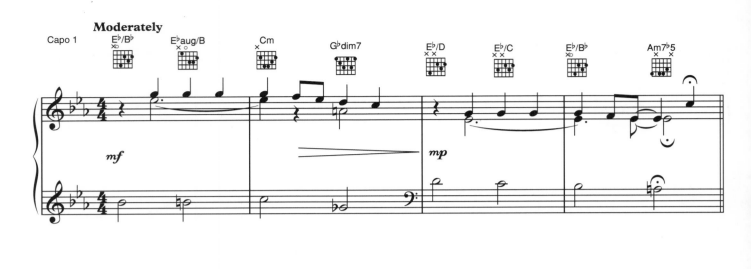

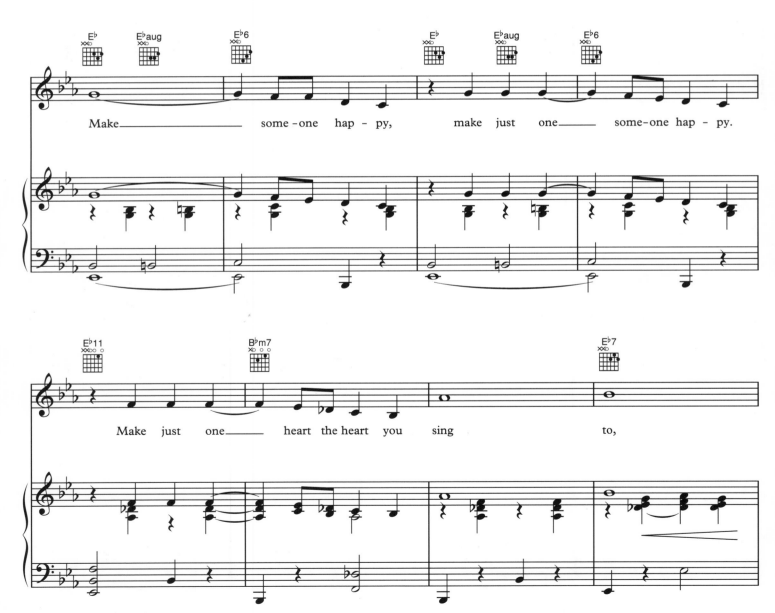

MOCKINGBIRD

Words and Music by CHARLIE FOXX and INEZ FOXX

why I keep on shout-in' in your ear— say-in' wo, wo, wo,— wo, wo.

repeat and fade

Verse 2:
Well, now, everybody have you heard?
She's gonna buy me a mockingbird
If that mockingbird don't sing
She's gonna buy me a diamond ring
And if that diamond ring won't shine
Guess it surely break this poor heart of mine
And that's the reason why I keep on tellin' everybody
Sayin' no, no, no, no, no, no, no, no

Verse 3:
Listen now and understand
She's gonna find me some peace of mind
And if that peace of mind won't stay
I'm gonna get myself a better way
I might rise above, I might go below
Ride with the tide and go with the flow
And if that's the reason why I keep on shouting in your ears, y'all
No, no, no, no, no, no, now, now, baby

MUSTANG SALLY

Words and Music by BONNY RICE

All you wan-na do is ride__ a-round, Sal - ly. *Ride Sal-ly__ ride.__*

All you wan-na do is ride__ a - round,__ Sal - ly. *Ride, Sal-ly__ ride.__*

All you wan - na do is ride__ a - round, Sal - ly. *Ride, Sal-ly__ ride.__*

One of these ear - ly morn - ings,

59

Verse 2:
I bought you a brand new Mustang
It was a nineteen sixty-five
Now you come around, signifying a woman
Girl, you won't, you won't let me ride
Mustang Sally, now baby
Guess you better slow that Mustang down
You been runnin' all over town
Oh, guess you gotta put your flat feet on the ground

MY KIND OF TOWN (CHICAGO IS)

Words by SAMMY CAHN
Music by JAMES VAN HEUSEN

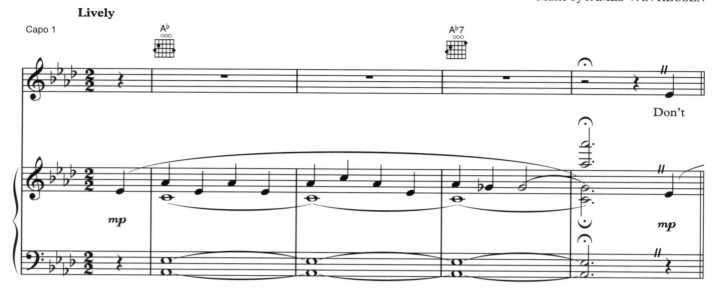

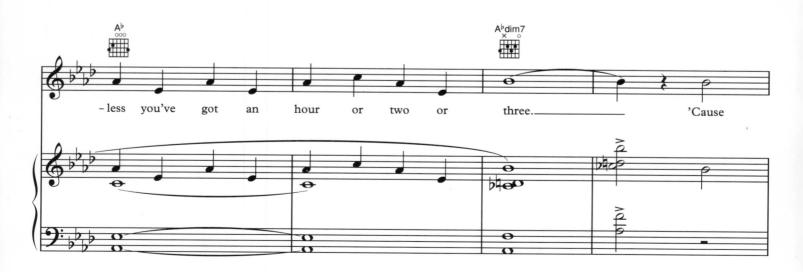

the   Wind - y   Ci - ty,   Chi - ca - go is,

the   Un - ion   Stock - yards,   Chi - ca - go is,

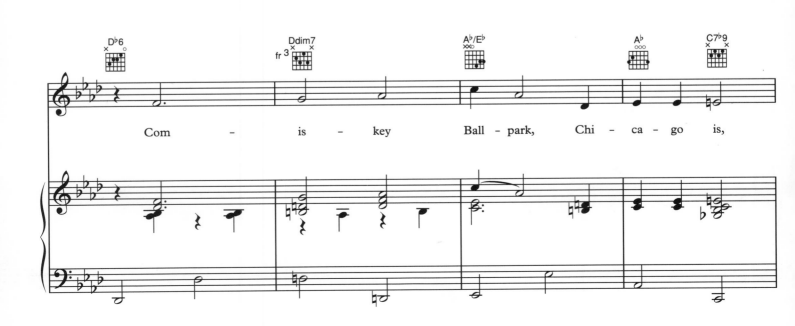

Com - is - key   Ball - park,   Chi - ca - go is,

THE NEXT TIME

Words and Music by BUDDY KAYE and PHILIP SPRINGER

ONE FINE DAY

Words and Music by GERRY GOFFIN and CAROLE KING

One fine day you'll look at me,

and you will know our love was meant to be.

One fine day you're gon-na want me for your

girl. Shoo-be-do-be-do-be - do-be-do wah, wah, shoo-be-do-be-do-be - do-be-do wah, wah.

repeat ad lib and fade

Verse 2:
The arms I long for will open wide
And you'll be proud to have me walking right by your side
One fine day you're gonna want me for your girl

Verse 3:
One fine day we'll meet once more
And then you'll want the love you threw away before
One fine day you're gonna want me for your girl

RESCUE ME

Words and Music by CARL SMITH and RAYNARD MINER

RUNAROUND SUE

Words and Music by DION DI MUCCI and ERNIE MARESCA

SITTING ON THE DOCK OF THE BAY

Words and Music by OTIS REDDING and STEVE CROPPER

Sit-tin' in the morn-ing sun, ___ I'll be sit-tin' 'til the eve-nin' ___ come,
Left my home in Geor-gia, head-ed for the Fris-co ___ Bay,
Sit-tin' here rest-in' my bones ___ and this lone-li-ness won't leave me a - lone.

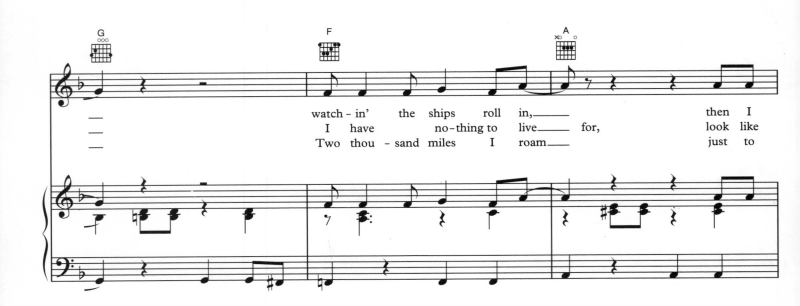

watch-in' the ships roll in, ___ then I
I have no-thing to live ___ for, look like
Two thou-sand miles I roam ___ just to

NO PARTICULAR PLACE TO GO

Words and Music by CHUCK BERRY

SUGAR SUGAR

Words and Music JEFF BARRY and ANDY KIM

SPANISH HARLEM

Words and Music by JERRY LEIBER and PHIL SPECTOR

There is a rose in Spa-nish Har - lem,

a rare rose up in Spa-nish Har - lem.

It is a spe-cial one, it's ne-ver seen the sun, it on-ly
With eyes as black as coal that look down in my soul and start a

comes up when the moon is on the run and all the stars are gleam-ing.
fire there and then I lose con-trol, I have to beg your par-don.

1.

It's grow-ing in the street right up through the con-crete, but soft and sound in

pale moon.

2.

I'm going to pick that rose and watch her as she grows

in my gar - den.

SUMMER WIND

German Words by HANS BRADTKE
English Words by JOHNNY MERCER
Music by HENRY MAYER

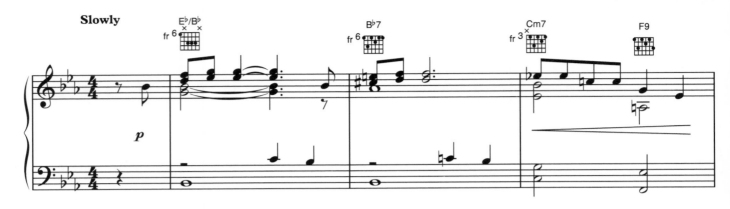

The sum-mer wind came blow-ing in a-cross the sea,— it

lin-gered there to touch your hair and walk with me.— All

still the days, the lone-ly days go on and on.— And guess who sighs his

lul-la-bies through nights that ne-ver end, my fick-le

friend, the sum-mer wind,— the sum-mer wind,— the sum-mer wind.

SWEET BABY JAMES

Words and Music by JAMES TAYLOR

SWEETS FOR MY SWEET

Words and Music by DOC POMUS and MORT SHUMAN

UNDER THE BOARDWALK

Words and Music by ARTIE RESNICK and KENNY YOUNG

SUNNY AFTERNOON

Words and Music by RAY DAVIES

The tax-man's tak-en all—— my dough, and left me in my
girl-friend's gone off with—— my car,—— and gone back to her

state-ly home; laz-ing on a sun-ny af-ter-noon—— and I can't sail
ma and pa;—— tel-ling tales of drunk-en-ness and cruel-ty.—— Now I'm sit-

—— my yacht, he's tak-en ev-'ry-thing I've got,——
-ting here—— sip-ping at my ice-cold beer,——

WATERMELON MAN

Words by GLORIA LYNNE
Music by HERBIE HANCOCK

WHERE DID OUR LOVE GO?

Words and Music by BRIAN HOLLAND, LAMONT DOZIER
and EDDIE HOLLAND

Ba — by, ba — by, ba — by don't leave me,
Ba — by, ba — by, where did our love go

ooh, please don't leave me all by my — self.
and all of your pro — mi — ses of a love for — ev — er more?

I've got this burn — ing, burn — ing, yearn — ing feel — ing in — side me,

WHEREVER I LAY MY HAT (THAT'S MY HOME)

Words and Music by NORMAN WHITFIELD, MARVIN GAYE
and BARRETT STRONG

look in your eye   I can tell you're gon - na cry,   is it ov - er   me?___
had a ro - mance,   did you break it   by chance   ov - er   me?___
I'm the type of guy   who gives a girl the eye   ev - 'ry - bo - dy   knows.

WILD THING

Words and Music by CHIP TAYLOR

WOULDN'T IT BE NICE

Words and Music by BRIAN WILSON, TONY ASHER
and MIKE LOVE

Would – n't it be nice if we were old – er?_____ Then we would – n't
nice if we could wake_____ up_____ in_____ the morn – ing

have to wait_____ so_____ long._____ And would – n't it be nice to live to – geth –
when the day_____ is_____ new?_____ And af – ter hav – ing spent the day to – geth –

it on - ly makes it worse to live with - out__ it_____ but let's talk a - bout

__ it. Oh would-n't it__ be__ nice?_____

repeat and fade

Good night,__ oh ba - by,
sleep tight,__ oh ba - by.

YOUNG GIRL

Words and Music by JERRY FULLER

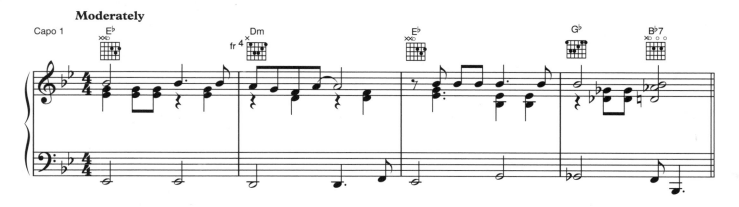

Young girl, get out of my mind. My love for you is way out of line.— Bet-ter

run, girl,_____ you're much too young, girl._____

With all the charms of a wo-man,
Be-neath your per - fume and make-up,
So hur – ry home to your ma - ma.

you've kept the
you're just a
I'm sure she

sec - ret of your youth.
ba - by in dis - guise.
won-ders where you are.

You led me
And though you
Get out of

to bel-ieve___ you're old en-ough to give me love,
know that it___ is wrong to be___ a - lone with me,___
here be-fore___ I have the time___ to change my mind,

and now it
that 'come on'
'cause I'm a -

(YOU MAKE ME FEEL LIKE) A NATURAL WOMAN

Words and Music by CAROLE KING, GERRY GOFFIN
and JERRY WEXLER

Lookin' out on the morning rain,—
When my soul was in the lost and found,—

I used to feel un-in-spired.—
you came a-long to claim it.

And when I knew I'd have to face a-no-ther day,—
I did-n't know just what was wrong with me,—

Lord, it made me feel so tired.—
'til your kiss helped me name it.

Be – fore the day I met you, life was so un – kind.
Now I'm no long – er doubt – ful of what I'm liv – ing for, 'cause

Your love was the key to my＿ peace of mind,＿ 'cause you make me＿
if I make you hap – py I don't need to do＿ more,＿

feel,＿ you make me＿ feel,＿ you make me＿

feel like a＿ na – tu – ral wo – man.

YOU'RE ALL I NEED TO GET BY

Words and Music by ASHFORD and SIMPSON

you're all I need,_____ you're all I need___ to get by._

All I need to get by.

Verse 2:
Like an eagle protects his nest, for you I'll do my best
Stand by you like a tree and dare anybody to try and move me
Darling, in you I found strength where I was torn down
Don't know what's in store, but together we can open any door
Just to do what's good for you and inspire you a little higher
I know you can make a man out of a soul that didn't have a goal
'Cause we, we got the right foundation
And with love and determination
You're all, you're all I want to strive for
And do a little more all
All the joys under the sun wrapped up into one
You're all I need, you're all I need to get by
All I need to get by

YOU'RE SIXTEEN, YOU'RE BEAUTIFUL (AND YOU'RE MINE)

Words and Music by ROBERT B SHERMAN and RICHARD M SHERMAN

Printed in Great Britain by Hobbs the Printers Ltd, Totton, Hampshire 12/97

70 YEARS OF POPULAR MUSIC

The 70 Years of Popular Music is a collection of 31 books, each containing 40 of your favourite hits from the beginning of the 1900s to the present day. The music is arranged for piano with lyrics and guitar chord boxes included.

1900-1920
Order Ref: 16407
Including: After You've Gone;
The Floral Dance;
I'm Forever Blowing Bubbles; Swanee

The Forties Part One
Order Ref: 09908
Including: Almost Like Being
In Love; Blueberry Hill; Let There Be Love;
My Foolish Heart; Tenderly

The Forties Part Two
Order Ref: 17715
Including: Don't Get Around Much Any
More; I Remember You; Mona Lisa;
That Old Black Magic

The Forties Part Three
Order Ref: 2275A
Including: Busy Doin' Nothing;
Stella By Starlight; Swinging On A Star;
You Make Me Feel So Young

The Forties Part Four
Order Ref: 5622A
Including: Anything You Can Do;
Choo Choo Ch'Boogie; Route 66;
Tico-Tico (Tico-Tico No Fuba)

The Seventies Part One
Order Ref: 09911
Including: Baker Street;
Don't Give Up On Us;
Hi Ho Silver Lining; If; Mandy;
Music; When I Need You

The Seventies Part Two
Order Ref: 17307
Including: Chanson D'Amour; Chiqu
Diamonds Are Forever; Isn't She Lo
Jolene; Lost In France

The Seventies Part Three
Order Ref: 3118A
Including: Annie's Song; Easy;
Hotel California; I Will Survive;
Killer Queen; With You I'm Born Ag

The Seventies Part Four
Order Ref: 5625A
Including: Ain't No Sunshine;
Boogie Wonderland; Dancing Queer
Lady Marmalade; Top Of The World

The Twenties Part One
Order Ref: 09906
Including: April Showers;
Crazy Rhythm;
Makin' Whoopee!; Tea For Two;
Yes Sir That's My Baby

The Twenties Part Two
Order Ref: 17713
Including: Ain't Misbehavin';
The Charleston;
My Blue Heaven; Side By Side;
Singin' In The Rain

The Twenties Part Three
Order Ref: 2273A
Including: Ain't She Sweet;
Baby Face; Don't Bring Lulu;
It Had To Be You;
Who's Sorry Now

The Twenties Part Four
Order Ref: 5620A
Including: Basin St Blues;
Indian Love Call;
Let's Do It (Let's Fall In Love);
Without A Song

The Fifties Part One
Order Ref: 09909
Including: Autumn Leaves; Diana;
The Green Door;
I Could Have Danced All Night;
When I Fall In Love

The Fifties Part Two
Order Ref: 17305
Including: All The Way; Cry Me A River;
High Hopes; La Bamba; Living Doll;
Only Sixteen; Volare

The Fifties Part Three
Order Ref: 2276A
Including: Come Fly With Me; I Love Paris;
Magic Moments; Mister Sandman; Misty;
Sing A Rainbow

The Fifties Part Four
Order Ref: 5623A
Including: Ain't That A Shame;
Book Of Love; Heartbreak Hotel;
Island In The Sun; Sisters; Smile

The Eighties Part One
Order Ref: 16005
Including: Ben; Endless Love; It's My
Let's Hear It For The Boy; Move Cl
We've Got Tonight

The Eighties Part Two
Order Ref: 16966
Including: Axel F; Coming Around Ag
Like A Virgin; Nikita; Separate Lives;
Take My Breath Away

The Eighties Part Three
Order Ref: 3119A
Including: Anything For You;
Being With You; Careless Whisper;
Come On Eileen; Tainted Love

The Eighties Part Four
Order Ref: 5626A
Including: Breakout;
Everything Must Change; Kids In Am
Lady In Red; Missing You; Superwom

The Thirties Part One
Order Ref: 09907
Including: All Of Me; A Foggy Day;
I Only Have Eyes For You;
September Song;
Smoke Gets In Your Eyes

The Thirties Part Two
Order Ref: 17714
Including: About A Quarter To Nine;
Blue Moon; The Glory Of Love;
Moonlight Serenade;
Over The Rainbow; Stardust

The Thirties Part Three
Order Ref: 2274A
Including: Begin The Beguine;
A Fine Romance;
Lazy Bones; My Funny Valentine;
Stormy Weather

The Thirties Part Four
Order Ref: 5621A
Including: But Not For Me;
Georgia On My Mind;
Jeepers Creepers;
My Baby Just Cares For Me

The Sixties Part One
Order Ref 09910
Including: Alfie; Congratulations;
I'm A Believer; Moon River; Puppet
On A String; Try To Remember

The Sixties Part Two
Order Ref: 17306
Including: Anyone Who Had A Heart;
Blowin' In The Wind; A Groovy Kind Of
Love; The Loco-motion

The Sixties Part Three
Order Ref: 3117A
Including: Apache; Black Is Black; C'Mon
Everybody; Everlasting Love;
Leader Of The Pack

The Sixties Part Four
Order Ref: 5624A
Including: Baby Love;
California Girls; Itchycoo Park; Mustang
Sally; Sugar Sugar; Wild Thing; Young Girl

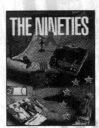

The Nineties Part One
Order Ref: 2277A
Including: All Woman; Get Here;
Heal The World; I Will Always Love
Promise Me; Sacrifice

The Nineties Part Two
Order Ref: 5627A
Including: All I Wanna Do; Breathe A
Don't Speak; Love Shack; Mmmbop;
Think Twice; Older

The 70 Years of Popular Music Series is available from all good music shops.

International Music Publications Limited
Southend Road, Woodford Green, Essex IG8 8HN, England
Tel: 0181 551 6131 Fax: 0181 551 9121 e-mail: IMP@dial.pipex.com